A Word from Dr. Bruce Wilkinson

DR. BRUCE H. WILKINSON is founder and president of Walk Thru the Bible Ministries.

One of the major goals of the "Master Your Money" Video Series is to encourage every participant to spend time with God every day by reading His Word and praying.

This *Master Your Money Devotional Guide*—specially prepared by Walk Thru the Bible Ministries—is designed to help you fulfill that goal personally for 30 days.

Each of the six video sessions is followed by five days of devotional readings to help you meditate again through the principles and Scriptures Ron Blue taught in the video lesson. What's more, every devotional includes an "Action Item" to help you put the truths to work in your life immediately.

If you watch the series week by week, you can read the five devotionals between sessions. Or if you watch the series all at once (during a weekend retreat or week-long series, for instance), you can read the devotionals in the 30 days following the course.

Spending time with the Lord every day by using these devotionals will help you make these lifechanging financial principles your own, and guide you to financial freedom as a wise steward of the resources God has entrusted to you. May the Lord bless you on your journey with Him.

Bruce H. Wilkinson

The Bottom Line

DAY 1

SESSION

1

Read
Psalm 95

The bottom line. That's a financial term that refers to the lowest line in a financial statement, showing net income or loss. But it can also refer to the "big idea" or "main point."

That's where we want to start in our devotional times with God. Because when you think about personal finances, you can easily become overwhelmed by the multitude of technical data, forms, and charts. But when you keep the bottom line of it all in mind, you'll never be intimidated by the details.

What is the bottom line of the "Master Your Money" Video Series? It's this: God owns it all.

He's the sovereign God of the universe, and that means everything that exists is His. It's in His hands. Under His authority.

The psalmist recognized God's ownership of everything: *For the Lord is the great God, and the great King above all gods. In His hand are the deep places of the earth; the heights of the hills are His also. The sea is His, for He made it; and His hands formed the dry land (Psalm 95:3-5).*

Haggai the prophet adds that God's possessions are even more specifically financial: *"The silver is Mine, and the gold is Mine," says the Lord of hosts (2:8).*

How should we respond to this truth? Listen to what the psalmist says after he affirms God's owner-ship: *Oh come, let us worship and bow down; let us kneel before the Lord our Maker. For He is our God, and we are the people of His pasture, and the sheep of His hand (Psalm 95:6-7).*

Worship and honor the God who owns it all. He holds every-thing in His hands—including your life. And how you live today as His steward will impact your eternity.

That truth is not intended to condemn, but to comfort. Because God loves and cherishes you more than anyone else could.

Trust Him. Acknowledge His ownership of all. Because that's the first step to financial freedom.

Action Item: Don't let God's ownership of everything remain a sterile theological fact. Let this truth sink in so deeply that it impacts every financial decision you make. Start by looking at the Asset Sheet in your *Workbook* (page 19). Pray over each line, giving God full authority over the items. After all, He has that authority whether you recognize it or not. Then mark through the title "Your Assets" and write at the top of the page, "God's Assets in My Care." Thank God for all He has blessed you with, and acknowledge anew His sovereignty in your life.

TODAY'S BOTTOM LINE

The first step to financial freedom is acknowledging that your loving, sovereign God owns it all.

Lighting the Way

Read

Matthew 5:13-16

If we focus our attention solely on the world's situation, we'll be frightened and frustrated every time.

That's why we need to keep in mind the truth of God's sovereignty and ownership over all things. Nothing that happens in our world—or will happen—ever surprises Him.

As His children, we're His representatives in the world. And our financial affairs impact our effectiveness in that role—perhaps more than we realize. If we're financially frightened and frustrated, it demonstrates we really aren't in tune with the God of the universe.

God sets forth in the Bible how we are to live as His representatives. Over the next three days we'll look at three roles He's designed for us.

First, we are to be salt and light: *"You are the salt of the earth. . . . You are the light of the world. . . . Let your light so shine before men, that they may see your good works and glorify your Father in heaven" (Matthew 5:13-16).*

Salt seasons. And believers season society with the truths of God's Kingdom, with the fruit of God's Spirit. Salt also creates thirst. So believers live in such a way that people are drawn to God, thirsting for His way in their own lives.

Light reveals. God's light is seen in our pure life. And that life in turn shows others the path to God.

What do salt and light have to do with finances? Just this: The things you buy, the money you give away, the way you handle your financial affairs, it all says a great deal to the world around you. And part of being salt and light in the world is being a good manager of God's resources.

If you follow God's principles of money management, you'll stand in stark contrast to the world's ways. And that's one great way to fulfill your role as salt and light.

Action Item: List the names of five non-Christians you know—neighbors, co-workers, friends. Now ask yourself some tough questions: How well do these people really know you? Have you shared yourself with them? Have you shared your Lord with them? If they were to look at your finances, what would they learn about you? How would your checkbook "witness" to them? The answers to those questions will help you answer this overriding question: *Am I being salt and light in my world?* Pray for the people on your list, asking God to help you be salt and light in their lives. That's a prayer He'll honor, because it's a privilege He loves to see us exercise.

TODAY'S BOTTOM LINE

God calls His children to be seasoning salt and illuminating light to reveal His way to the world.

A Servant's Heart

DAY 3
SESSION 1

Read
Mark 10:43-45

Servanthood is not a popular occupation these days. It's a dirty job. It's demeaning. And it doesn't pay too well, either!

Yet God calls His children to be servants. That's not an option—it's a command.

The problem is, we rebel at the thought of being a servant. Sure, it sounds like a nice, pious idea. But it's not something we want to actually apply to our lives.

The fact is, the blessings of servanthood—now and throughout eternity—will far surpass those we'd receive by living any other way.

Jesus is our example of servanthood. He said: *"Whoever desires to become great among you shall be your servant. And whoever of you desires to be first shall be slave of all. For even the Son of Man did not come to be served, but to serve, and to give His life a ransom for many" (Mark 10:43-45).*

It's a paradox that many will never fully grasp: The path to greatness is the path of the servant. Jesus illuminated that path by His very life. The great and awesome God, who created the universe, came to live among His creatures as a man. Not as a taskmaster, nor a tyrant, but as a servant. A servant unto death.

It boggles the mind. Yet, if *He* could do it—and do it gladly—surely *we* can.

Paul the Apostle encourages us likewise: *For though I am free from all men, I have made myself a servant to all, that I might win the more (1 Corinthians 9:19).*

Why did Paul make himself a servant? *"That I might win the more."* You see, our servanthood is a means of shining the light to others around us, who will see that our lives are distinctive because they're godly.

Servant of God, accept the challenge your Master has set before you. It's a mindset that will revolutionize your life. And your world.

Action Item: Money is one of the most significant resources with which Christians can serve others. Hundreds of Christians are serving others by giving fortunes away. How can you become a servant through your finances? First, meditate on the example of Christ by spending some time reading Philippians 2:1-11. Think how that mindset in your life would change your financial habits. What would you give up? How would you spend your money differently? How could you serve others through your financial gifts? As you think and pray, jot down your thoughts. Perhaps God is just waiting to give you some great ideas!

TODAY'S BOTTOM LINE

God calls His children to be servants to a hurting, needy world ...just like His Son.

A Faithful Steward

DAY 4

SESSION 1

Read
1 Corinthians 4:1-2

You don't hear the word "steward" much today. Even flight attendants don't like to be called "stewardesses" anymore!

Consequently it's not easy for people today to grasp the meaning of the word. It's just not part of our daily vocabulary.

So what is a steward? One who manages another person's property. He's not an owner who has *rights*; he's a manager who has *responsibilities*.

The Bible says that, whether we realize it or not, each of us is a steward of another person's property. Whose property? God's—because He owns it all.

That stewardship involves not only the Good News of Jesus Christ, which He entrusts to His children to pass along, but all the tangible assets of our lives as well.

In Bible times, just as today, owners would often entrust the management of their properties or assets to professional stewards. Obviously, the steward had to perform faithfully and proficiently, or he wouldn't last long in his job.

The same is true for believers, as Paul writes: *Let a man so consider us, as servants of Christ and stewards of the mysteries of God. Moreover it is required in stewards that one be found faithful (1 Corinthians 4:1-2).*

Stewards must be found faithful. That means they must manage what is entrusted to them in the most effective way possible for their master. In our case as believers, the Owner is the One who has purchased us with His blood.

If any steward should be faithful to his master, it should be the Christian, whose Master loves him and desires the best for him.

This course is designed to help you become the best, most faithful steward you can be. For His glory.

Action Item: Ron Blue defined stewardship as "the use of God-given resources for the accomplishment of God-given goals." Every resource or possession we have has been entrusted to us by its true Owner, God. He has placed us in the role of a steward to manage the part of His "estate" that He's given us. And we are to use those resources to accomplish the goals He has set for us. Later we'll think more carefully about our goals. For now, try to list the top three financial goals of your life. Do you sense they are indeed *God's* goals for you? If so, in what ways are you managing your resources right now to accomplish those goals? If not, spend some time in prayer. Ask God to give you the goals He'd have you pursue as His child.

TODAY'S BOTTOM LINE

God calls His children to be stewards, faithfully managing the resources He entrusts to us.

Important Implications

The concepts we've reviewed these past few days are certainly not new. Nor are they difficult to understand. But they can be revolutionary.

Let's think through them again by focusing on a story Jesus told: the Parable of the Talents. Read it for yourself in Matthew 25:14-30, because it can illuminate some of the basic Biblical principles of money management we've discovered so far in this series.

First: God owns it all (see Matthew 25:14). Very few Christians would argue with that principle. And yet its implications are revolutionary.

Second: We are in a growth process (see Matthew 25:21). Our time on earth is temporary and is used by our Lord as a time of training, with the goal that we are formed into the image of His Son, Jesus.

Third: The amount is not important (see Matthew 25:23). Compare verses 21 and 23 and you'll see that the master's commendation was identical, no matter how much the steward started with. That indicates that the amount you have is unimportant. But how you handle that amount is vitally important.

Fourth: Faith requires action (see Matthew 25:24-30). The wicked slave knew what he should do, but did nothing. Many of us know what we ought to do, but we disobey. Or we delay. We are so bombarded by worldly input that we are paralyzed. We take no action for fear of making a mistake Biblically or financially. Or we're frustrated and confused. We need to learn a lesson from the wicked servant's fate: God wants *active* stewards.

Those are four crucial concepts to nail down before you can fully understand how to master your money. And when you do, you can look forward to the Lord saying: *"Well done, good and faithful servant; you were faithful over a few things, I will make you ruler over many things. Enter into the joy of your lord"* (Matthew 25:21).

Action Item: If you own your own home, take a walk around your property to get a feel for the reality of these principles. Reflect on how long that dirt has been there. And how long it will continue to be there. (If you don't own your home, take inventory of the things you do own.) Then ask yourself if you really own it or merely possess it. You may have the title to it, but that title reflects your right to possess it temporarily, not forever. Only God literally owns it forever. Really believing this frees us to give generously of God's resources to God's purposes and God's people.

TODAY'S BOTTOM LINE

Financial freedom begins when we understand our role as a steward of God's resources.

Little by Little

DAY 1

SESSION 2

Read
Proverbs 13:11

When God created the world, He chose not to make a money tree. He no doubt exercised great wisdom in doing so, or else we'd have to spend a lot of time literally raking in the money!

Even so, there is a phenomenon in money management that makes it seem as though money is growing on trees.

It's called the "magic of compounding."

You may remember the charts we looked at in Session 2 (see pages 28 and 29 in the *Course Workbook*). Those may appear to be rather boring columns of digits, but in actuality they reveal a principle that can create an incredible balance sheet over time.

It's not surprising to realize that this principle has its source in God's Word. Solomon talks about it in Proverbs: *Dishonest money dwindles away, but he who gathers money little by little makes it grow (Proverbs 13:11 NIV).*

Did you catch the basic concept there? Gather money little by little, and thereby make it grow.

That's precisely what compounding does. Whether you start with $100 or $1,000 or $10,000 or more, the results over time invested at a reasonable rate can be phenomenal.

As stewards, we're charged to manage God's resources as efficiently and effectively as possible. The parable of the talents (Matthew 25), which we read earlier, indicates that investing money wisely—and reaping the benefits financially—is a practice God encourages.

And that makes the magic of compounding a concept that's crucial for Christians to understand . . . and put to work.

Action Item: Look again at the charts on pages 28 and 29 in the *Course Workbook,* and think about the savings programs you have—perhaps a passbook account, a money market fund, or stocks and bonds. In light of your long-term goals (which may include retirement, college educations for the kids, owning your own business, or special giving), how close are you to where you'd like to be? Perhaps you haven't really thought through your goals—we'll do that in Session 3. Even so, try to locate where you'd like to be financially on those charts when you hit retirement. What would it take to get there? Close by asking God in prayer to keep your financial future in perspective, according to His will for you.

TODAY'S BOTTOM LINE

Compounding is a financial tool that helps us manage God's resources responsibly.

Success Story

DAY 2

SESSION 2

Read
Isaiah 55:8

One time a retired pastor came to Ron Blue with a concern about whether he had enough to pay for his wife's nursing home care. He'd never made more than $8,000 in a year, had retired about 20 years before, and now faced some rather frightening financial prospects.

Yet when they went through the planning process, Ron discovered the man had accumulated $1,663,000 in liquid assets! How? By taking advantage of the magic of compounding and investing years earlier . . . and by following the three principles of financial success discussed in Session 2. Remember?

1. *Spend less than you earn over the long term.* In other words, live within your means. The pastor followed this principle and built up a nest egg which he could invest profitably. This isn't easy. It requires faithfulness—a rare commodity.

2. *Remember the opportunity cost of consumption.* If you buy something you really don't need, you aren't just losing the amount of money it cost—you're losing what that amount could have grown to over time with compounding.

3. *Consider the cost of making a mistake.* A major purchase that is financially foolish—buying a new car you really don't need, for instance—costs you far more than the price you pay. To avoid making such costly mistakes, spend time with God to determine His will for you in your financial affairs.

These basic principles can bring tremendous benefits in the long run. Yet they are rarely followed today. And that's why there's so much financial hardship. As Isaiah reminds us: *"My thoughts are not your thoughts, nor are your ways My ways,"* says the Lord (Isaiah 55:8). That truth is abundantly evident in the financial area, isn't it?

The principles are clear. They work. And they bring true financial freedom, God's way!

Action Item: Think about the last major purchase you made—a car, furniture, or major appliance. Look at it right now, and ask yourself: Are you enjoying it? Is it still "brand new"? What were the reasons you bought it? Looking back, in light of the three principles we reviewed today, do you think it was a wise purchase? Well, the past is history—you can't undo those decisions. But you can start following these financial principles *today*, and look forward to financial freedom *tomorrow*. If that's your commitment, tell God about it right now. Then write your initials and today's date on this page.

TODAY'S BOTTOM LINE

The Bible's principles of financial success may not be easy to obey, but they work.

Dangers of Debt

Read
James 4:13-17

Debt. The world tells you one thing. The Bible, something entirely different.

The world says credit is an important part of your financial identity. The more credit cards you have, the better your lifestyle can be. *Anything* is within your grasp if you can simply get the payments low enough. But the Bible says, *Owe no one anything except to love one another (Romans 13:8).*

The Bible never calls *borrowing* a sin. Rather, the sin is *not repaying.* In fact, one who fails to repay is called "wicked" in Psalm 32:21.

Even so, God's people should never put themselves in a position where they might unexpectedly fall into sin. And borrowing with no guaranteed way to repay only opens the way to do so.

As we learned in Session 2, debt has two primary dangers.

First, *debt always presumes upon the future.* If you go into debt, as a Christian you are obligated to repay—yet you take on that obligation without knowing for certain whether you will be able to repay or not. As James instructs us: *Come now, you who say, "Today or tomorrow we will go to such and such a city, spend a year there, buy and sell, and make a profit"; whereas you do not know what will happen tomorrow. For what is your life? It is even a vapor that appears for a little time and then vanishes away. Instead you ought to say, "If the Lord wills, we shall live and do this or that." But now you boast in your arrogance. All such boasting is evil (James 4:13-17).*

Second, *debt may deny God an opportunity to work.* For instance, if Ron Blue had funded the start-up of his Christian financial planning practice the "normal" way through a line of credit, he's convinced he would have prevented God from providing the necessary funds—as He miraculously did!

Remember, our ways are not necessarily God's ways. Trust Him for your needs, then watch Him go to work on your behalf.

Action Item: Open your wallet or purse and remove all the credit cards you carry with you. Lay them all out before you. Think through how much you owe on each card. Add it all up (if it's zero, we salute you!). Without even considering your consumer debt, auto loans, etc., ask yourself how dangerous your debt situation is—in light of what we've learned. Is God meeting your needs in unusual ways? Or are you not giving Him the opportunity to do so? Before you put those credit cards back in your wallet . . . consider putting them elsewhere!

TODAY'S BOTTOM LINE

Debt—the flip side of compounding—works against you both financially and spiritually.

The Root Problem

DAY 4

SESSION 2

Read Luke 12:15

Pick up any newspaper's business section and you'll probably read about the failure of a major company, caused by a crushing burden of debt through which it overextended itself.

But the personal failures—men and women financially devastated by debt—don't usually make the newspapers. Yet they're just as true . . . and even more tragic.

God reminds us, however, that debt is never the real problem. As Jesus said, *"Take heed and beware of covetousness, for one's life does not consist in the abundance of the things he possesses" (Luke 12:15).* Debt is only symptomatic of the real problem: greed, self-indulgence, impatience, fear, poor self-image, lack of self-worth, lack of self-discipline, or something else.

When we experience problems like those, we try to patch them over with something that can ease our pain quickly, rather than trust in God and rely on His provision. But that only feeds the root problem. It never solves anything.

These four implications of debt make its danger clear:

1. Compounding works against you. Compounding can enlarge your investment amazingly over time. But the same principle can work *against* you—when *you're* the one who must pay the growing interest.

2. Getting in debt is easier than getting out. If you're overspending by $1,000 a year, then you must not only *stop* overspending, but also *start* paying it back with interest. That's difficult. But it can be done, little by little over a long time.

3. Debt mortgages the future. Because of the interest payments you must make, you are sentencing yourself to a lower standard of living in the future.

4. Debt robs you of the freedom of choice. You have an obligation to repay—it becomes your number one financial priority.

Rather than using debt to solve our problems—and finding ourselves in greater jeopardy than before—God invites us to place ourselves in His hands.

Action Item: Meditate again on Jesus' words in Luke 12:15. Then turn to Matthew 6:24-34 and read it twice. Let those Scriptures lead you into a time of soul-searching with your Lord. As you pray, rededicate yourself to following the Lord in your finances. Commit yourself to avoid the use of debt, and to take steps now to get out of debt. Close your time by praising your Father for His loving care, no matter how desperate your situation may be.

TODAY'S BOTTOM LINE

Debt—a symptom of much deeper problems—keeps us from experiencing God's best for us.

5 Steps to Freedom

Several years ago on a plane trip Ron Blue sat next to a distinguished looking gentleman. The man asked Ron what he did for a living.

Ron told him about his financial planning practice based on Biblical principles, and summarized the five key steps to financial success he had derived from his study of God's Word. The man listened intently, agreeing that each one was crucial.

Ron was feeling pretty good about himself, sharing his wisdom with this man. Imagine his chagrin when he discovered the man was chairman of the House Ways and Means Committee—a financial expert if there ever was one!

Even so, his assessment of the principles Ron teaches was "right on the money." He recognized that God's principles are true . . . even if most people—and the government itself—rarely follow them.

Here are those five keys to financial success:

1. *Understand the Biblical principles.* Your involvement in this series shows you've made a commitment to know God's will for your financial life.

2. *Adopt a nonconsumptive lifestyle.* Live simply, frugally. Make saving a priority to enable you to reach the financial goals God sets before you.

3. *Avoid the use of debt.* As we've seen, nothing is more destructive to your financial health than debt.

4. *Keep your liquidity high.* As we'll see in Session 4, a wise inves-tor follows a step-by-step strategy. The first steps involve making sure you have adequate emergency funds (liquid assets) you can use quickly.

5. *Set long-term goals.* In our next session we'll learn how to set goals that are godly and achievable. Because if you aim at nothing, you'll hit it every time.

These keys will enable you to fulfill the responsibility God has set before you: *If anyone does not provide for his own, and especially for those of his household, he has denied the faith and is worse than an unbeliever (1 Timothy 5:8).*

God is prepared to help you meet that responsibility in every way possible.

Action Item: Look again at those five keys listed above. Put a checkmark beside the ones you feel you are currently following. Are you satisfied with the number of checkmarks? If not, ask God to use the remaining sessions of this series to impress His truth on your life. To make His principles real. To give you the strength and wisdom to apply them every day. That's a prayer He'll gladly answer.

TODAY'S BOTTOM LINE

God's simple but radical financial principles can lead to solid stewardship and financial freedom.

The Ant's Example

DAY 1

SESSION 3

Read
Proverbs 21:5

A study of Harvard graduates with MBA degrees revealed that 3% of them accomplished more than the other 97% combined. The only differentiating characteristic was that the 3% had left Harvard with written goals.

Setting goals is a practice God encourages His children to follow. Not that we should be overly specific and unalterably tied to our goals, thereby possibly missing God's will for us. But the call for aim in life is clear.

As Solomon tells us: *The ants are a people not strong, yet they prepare their food in the summer (Proverbs 30:25; see also 6:6-8).* Look at the ant and learn to plan ahead . . . and then work toward your plan.

Why? Proverbs answers: *The plans of the diligent lead surely to plenty, but those of everyone who is hasty, surely to poverty (Proverbs 21:5).*

Setting goals carefully and following them diligently brings rewarding benefits. It's all part of the lifestyle of stewardship we're building.

• *Goals provide direction and purpose.* Unless we know where we're going, or why we're here, we may never accomplish anything.

• *Goals help us crystallize our thinking.* Until we wrestle with our purpose and aims in life, we may never really understand why God has placed us here. The process of setting goals can be freeing.

• *Goals provide personal motivation.* Whether short- or long-term, goals provide a focus that can energize us.

• *Goals are a statement of God's will for your life.* Through prayer and Bible study, we can come to some conclusions—though certainly not to be set in concrete—that in effect indicate where we think God may be leading us in the future.

Remember our definition of stewardship: "Using God-given resources to accomplish God-given goals." Having goals is half the job. Without goals, we cannot be godly stewards.

Action Item: Think back to your childhood, and jot down some of the goals you had then. For instance, do you remember what you wanted to be when you grew up? Did you make it? Perhaps not, but even so, think how even the childish goals you had then influenced your life, giving you hope, purpose, and encouragement. Do you have goals now? Prepare yourself through prayer right now to get into the process of goal-setting this week. Ask God for His guidance as you do.

TODAY'S BOTTOM LINE

Setting goals carefully and following them diligently brings rewarding benefits to God's stewards.

Counting the Cost

Jesus encouraged the multitudes to count the cost of discipleship. And in so doing, He confronted us with the need for planning and goals.

He said: *"For which of you, intending to build a tower, does not sit down first and count the cost, whether he has enough to finish it—lest, after he has laid the foundation, and is not able to finish it, all who see it begin to mock him, saying, 'This man began to build and was not able to finish'"* (Luke 14:28-30).

Without goals, we may end up with a lifetime of false starts, unable to achieve anything of substance, surrounded by unfinished memorials to our good intentions.

So why don't we set goals? As we learned in Session 3, there are several common reasons.

1. I don't want to fail. If you don't set a goal, you won't fail to meet it. And failure is not an enjoyable experience. But Jesus reminds us that the very process of planning is what keeps us from a life of failures. Without specific goals to aim for, Jesus' words could apply to us: *"This man began to build and was not able to finish."* Setting reasonable goals doesn't guarantee that we'll complete them, of course. But it certainly helps the process.

2. I don't have time. Some people claim they're too busy to go through the goal-setting and planning process. But that's not valid. Everyone has goals and dreams—but they are often nebulous. By recording them, you bring them much closer to reality.

3. I don't know what goals to set. Obviously, it's crucial to set goals according to God's will. This means we must know the mind of God. How? We'll find out tomorrow.

4. I don't know how to set goals. We worked through the steps in Session 3, and we'll review them through these devotionals this week. Perhaps this will give you the guidance you need to succeed.

One of the major reasons the church today seems so powerless in society is that believers lack goals . . . which means they rarely achieve anything of importance, and simply get lost in the shuffle. Don't let that be said of you. Stand out for God!

Action Item: As you think through the four common reasons we don't set goals, which one(s) do you identify with most? Knowing what you know now, what specific steps will you take to overcome that obstacle to goal-setting? Write down the actions you'll take, then ask God to give you the strength and the wisdom you need to carry them out this week.

TODAY'S BOTTOM LINE

We must overcome the obstacles to setting goals if we are to succeed as God's stewards.

A "New Thing"

God's words in Isaiah 43:18-19 are comforting. Of course, they relate to Israel's promised restoration, but they also picture His desire for us:

"Do not remember the former things, nor consider the things of old. Behold, I will do a new thing, now it shall spring forth; shall you not know it?" (Isaiah 43:18-19).

God wants to do a new thing in each of our lives. And the process of setting goals under His direction can get us started on that path.

How? Here are the "don'ts":

1. *Don't focus on past failures.* Remember, God is *able to do exceedingly abundantly above all that we ask or think, according to the power that works in us (Ephesians 3:20).* Prepare to take new steps in the power of God's Spirit.

2. *Don't focus on present resources.* If your goals depend on what you have now, they will no doubt be insignificant or unachievable. God possesses all resources, so don't limit your dreams unnecessarily.

3. *Don't set goals apart from your spouse.* To be achievable, goals require "joint ownership" by husband and wife. Both need to pull together to reach them.

Here's the flipside—the "do's" of setting goals:

1. Above all, *spend time with God.* If you were to read only one good piece of financial planning advice, this would be it. It's the foundation on which everything we do rests. That's why we included these devotionals, to give you the opportunity to read, meditate, and pray, offering you "jumping off places" for your own times with God.

2. *Record your goals.* Write them down. Review them. This gives you something solid to shoot for, not nebulous thoughts you'll never hit.

3. *Make your goals measurable.* Quantify them—set specific amounts and dates. The more concrete you are, the more confident you can be of reaching your goals.

Those may be simple "do's and don'ts." But they can have profound consequences.

Action Item: If you haven't yet done so, now is the time to begin setting your goals. You may need to spend several hours in the process. In fact, if you're married, it may be a good idea to get away somewhere far from the routine hassles to pray and plan together. If that's not possible, at least spend a weekend at home involved in the process. Not only will you be on your way to financial freedom, but you just might enjoy getting to know each other even better!

TODAY'S BOTTOM LINE

God is prepared to do a "new thing" in our lives as we set specific goals with His guidance.

The First Step

DAY 4

SESSION 3

Read
Hebrews 11:7-8

There's a danger associated with goal-setting. That danger is to spend a lot of time working through your goals, writing them down, praying over them . . . and then doing nothing about them!

That makes setting goals merely a mental exercise, rather than a guide toward financial freedom.

Faith, after all, is an action. So a faith goal means you act on what you believe God wants you to do.

Two points are crucial here. First, it's *God's responsibility* to provide the resources we need to meet the goals He's led us to establish. And second, it's *our responsibility* to take the first step.

That may not be easy. But Hebrews 11 can encourage us to get going.

For instance, consider Noah. *By faith Noah, being divinely warned of things not yet seen, moved with godly fear, prepared an ark for the saving of his household, by which he condemned the world and became heir of the righteousness which is according to faith (Hebrews 11:7).*

Had Noah ever seen rain? No. So why was he building an ark? That was pretty foolish, on the face of it. And it took him 100 years to complete. But it was a goal God had specifically given him.

It's clear that Noah's faith was strong. He had spent time with God, and he had a specific goal. An unshakable goal. A goal only God could help him reach.

Then there's Abraham: *By faith Abraham obeyed when he was called to go out to the place which he would afterward receive as an inheritance. And he went out, not knowing where he was going (11:8).*

That's faith. And it called for action: obedience to God's call.

Hebrews 11 is full of examples of strong faith. They all encourage us to spend time with God, set a goal, then take the first step—no matter how small it may seem.

Action Item: What small step will you take today toward your goal? Maybe it's paying an additional $25 this month on your credit card debt. Or cutting up the credit card itself. Maybe it's postponing that home purchase. Or selling the new car you have and buying a dependable used model. Or making a commitment to tithe regularly. Whatever it may be, take the first step. You may not be able to see how you will do it, but God will give you the encouragement you need. If you need an extra nudge, remember Ephesians 3:20—God is able to do exceedingly abundantly above all that we ask or think.

TODAY'S BOTTOM LINE

God calls His children to take the first step toward accomplishing our goals by faith.

Reaching the Goal

Whenever you get overwhelmed by the prospects of meeting a major goal you've set, think about Nehemiah. When he learned about the disrepair of Jerusalem and the distress of the people who had returned from captivity, their burden became his. Without the protection of city walls, the people faced almost certain doom.

Immediately Nehemiah turned to God in prayer—then he took the first step. He boldly approached the king and asked to be sent to Jerusalem to rebuild the walls. Though the king would miss Nehemiah's valued counsel as cupbearer, he permitted him to go.

But that was the easy part. Now Nehemiah faced a mammoth task, which had to be completed swiftly in the face of intense opposition from neighboring enemies.

The goal was gigantic. But it was God-given. So. . . *the wall was finished on the twenty-fifth day of the month of Elul, in fifty-two days. And it happened, when all our enemies heard of it, and all the nations around us saw these things, that they were very dis-heartened in their own eyes; for they perceived that this work was done by our God (Nehemiah 6:15-16).*

From Nehemiah's example we can draw great encouragement. From his experience we can note three results of faith goal setting:

1. The goal will be reached. Why? Because it's God's goal. He will move heaven and earth to perform His will. In His eyes it has already been accomplished.

2. Growth will be experienced. When you see God working to meet His goals, your faith in Him will grow.

3. God will be glorified. Obviously, He is the One who accomplishes our goals. And to Him belong praise and honor for it.

The Bible is full of examples of people like us who trusted God for their big dreams. Maybe you can provide an example that's just as dramatic for your world today—by His power, and for His glory.

Action Item: Goals involve every area of our life: lifestyle, debt, giving, taxes, accumulation, and so on. And the more comprehensive your goals are, relating to every area of your life, the more focused your life will be. Think again about the goals you've established this week. Have you "covered the bases" of your life? Have you pushed the limits beyond what is reasonable to expect, thus leaving plenty of room for God to work? If not, now's the time to rethink your goals. And then to step out in bold faith.

TODAY'S BOTTOM LINE

Goals can be achieved in God's power and for His glory when they are set by faith according to His will.

Seek God First

DAY 1

4

Read
Matthew 6:25-33

We've taken some important steps together so far in the "Master Your Money" Video Series.

First, we've come to understand that *God owns it all,* and that He has called us to be stewards of His resources.

Second, we've discovered the *magic of compounding,* which works positively in investments and negatively in debt.

Third, we've learned the *importance of setting goals.*

At this point, you may have developed some great financial goals—to get out of debt, begin to tithe, save for retirement, etc. And you may be wondering, "How do I pay for these wonderful goals I've established?" Good question!

As we learned in Session 4, you can reduce your lifestyle, your debt, and your taxes in order to increase your cash flow and fund your goals.

No one ever said it would be easy. It takes commitment, diligence, and sacrifice. But the rewards in the long run far outweigh the inconveniences now.

In this week's devotionals you'll be challenged to personalize what you've learned, to live more *simply* so you can live more *successfully* in God's eyes.

You may be a bit skeptical of this, or even worried about how you can pull it off. How you can continue to meet your obligations, cut back on expenses, and put off some purchases until you can fund them without credit.

But meditate on these words of Jesus Christ:

"Therefore I say to you, do not worry about your life, what you will eat or what you will drink; nor about your body, what you will put on. Is not life more than food and the body more than clothing? Look at the birds of the air, for they neither sow nor reap nor gather into barns; yet your heavenly Father feeds them. Are you not of more value than they? Which of you by worrying can add one cubit to his stature? . . . Therefore do not worry, saying, 'What shall we eat?' or 'What shall we drink?' or 'What shall we wear?' For after all these things the Gentiles seek. For your heavenly Father knows that you need all these things. But seek first the kingdom of God and His righteousness, and all these things shall be added to you" (Matthew 6:25-33).

Action Item: Why not spend a few moments memorizing Matthew 6:33 above. Let its truth sink in as you approach the subject of reducing your expenses. It's not just an empty set of words. It's a promise from the God of the universe!

TODAY'S BOTTOM LINE

When our priorities are properly set, God promises to meet every need of our life.

Living Simply

DAY 2

SESSION

4

**Read
Hebrews 13:5**

Ron Blue counsels with people who make less than $20,000 a year, others who make several million, and still others who make anything in between. You may find it hard to believe, but many of them struggle with the same problem: They can't make ends meet.

You see, *income* is not the problem. *Spending more than one's income* is the problem. So *reducing living expenses* is the first step to finding money you never knew you had.

It's common these days to seek the trappings of success—a high-priced watch, a snazzy sports car, an elegant home—without being able to afford it. Ron once noticed a man purchase on credit a watch costing thousands of dollars. The man even put the down payment on a credit card. When he walked out of the store and saw his first friend, what do you think the reaction would be? "Wow, Joe must be doing pretty well, because he can afford that expensive watch!" But Joe was wondering how he could make the payments on it for the next two years!

Our society has bankrupted itself by recklessly pursuing wealth on the dangerous road of credit. We buy certain material possessions to make a *statement*—which, unfortunately, is usually a *lie*.

Instead, as Christians we need to heed this verse: *A little that a righteous man has is better than the riches of many wicked (Psalm 37:16).* That may be hard for the world to understand, but we know it's true.

The Bible exhorts us, *Let your conduct be without covetousness, and be content with such things as you have. For He Himself has said, "I will never leave you nor forsake you" (Hebrews 13:5).* Notice the promise God makes here in relation to our contentment and lack of covetousness: He'll never leave us! He'll always be there to meet our needs.

Will you trust Him enough to believe that?

Action Item: You can reduce your lifestyle expenses. For instance, make sure you've established a realistic budget, then follow it. Go through your Projected Living Expenses forms (pages 42-43) item by item to trim expenditures, recognizing that every dollar saved goes directly into your cash flow. Finally, make yourself accountable to someone spiritually mature—your pastor or church leader, for instance—to avoid impulse purchases. None of these steps is easy, but you'll discover how beneficial they are for yourself. As soon as you begin to follow them.

TODAY'S BOTTOM LINE

We can reduce our lifestyle expenses by committing to live more simply and trusting God for our needs.

Living Debt-Free

DAY 3

SESSION 4

Read
Proverbs 22:7

When you use a credit card, studies have shown you'll spend on average 34% more than if you only use cash for purchases.

Credit card companies know this; that's why they make it so easy for you to get that card in your hands. Its presence in your wallet virtually assures that you will purchase things you never would have otherwise!

Therefore, *reducing debt* is a second major step you can take to find money you never knew you had. How?

First of all, establish a spending plan—a budget—to avoid the use of credit. Second, sell off assets you could do without to pay off outstanding debt. And third, follow the four criteria we discussed in Session 4 to decide whether to use debt. Let's review those criteria:

• *Economic:* Two rules come into play here. One, the return on whatever you are borrowing for must be greater than the cost of the debt. And two, you must have a guaranteed way to repay the debt. Most people figure their income is the "guaranteed" way to repay. But that's presuming upon the future.

• *Spiritual:* After spending time with God, if you still have a conviction that He would have you go into this debt, then you are free to proceed to the next criterion.

• *Psychological:* This is the peace-of-mind factor. Does it "feel right" to borrow the money? Or do you sense an added burden and tension at the prospect of owing more?

• *Marital:* Both spouses must have perfect unity that they are making the right decision to go into debt. That's the way marriage is supposed to work in God's eyes.

The best advice? Avoid debt. Stop using credit cards, and start paying them off. It may take a long time, but don't let that discourage you. God is prepared to help you through the process.

The Bible pulls no punches when it says: *The rich rules over the poor, and the borrower is servant to the lender (Proverbs 22:7).* Debt puts you in bondage to people and institutions who have only their profit—not yours—in mind. But you know that God has your best interests at heart. And being His servant is true freedom indeed.

Action Item: Work through those four criteria right now with a purchase you are considering. Get into the habit of considering these four checkpoints whenever you think about pulling out a credit card or filling out a loan application. It's a habit that will lead to good financial health.

TODAY'S BOTTOM LINE

We can reduce our debt and increase our cash flow by avoiding the bondage of credit and trusting God instead.

Our Fair Share

DAY 4
SESSION
4

Read
Romans 13:1,7

There's one expense we all would love to decrease: our taxes. But beware these pitfalls in the process of *reducing your taxes.*

• First pitfall is *making tax reduction a priority.* That will consume much time and energy but little difference financially in the long run.

• Second pitfall is *having a short-term perspective.* You should know at least a year in advance what your taxes will be.

• Third pitfall is *getting a tax refund.* It shows you have not planned well. Many people use their withholding as forced savings. But that's just poor stewardship.

If you avoid those three pitfalls, then you can cut your taxes with these two guaranteed methods. First, *earn less money.* With a lower income, you pay lower taxes. Second, *increase your expenses.* In other words, have more interest to deduct, greater charitable contributions, more business deductions, etc. But both of those "guaranteed ways" actually *cost* you money!

Above all, keep in mind what the Bible says about our responsibility: *Let every soul be subject to the governing authorities. For there is no authority except from God, and the authorities that exist are appointed by God. . . . Render therefore to all their due: taxes to whom taxes are due,* *customs to whom customs, fear to whom fear, honor to whom honor (Romans 13:1,7).*

God has sovereignly established the authorities of this world. Paul wrote those verses while Nero—a pagan if there ever was one—ruled the Roman Empire. Yet Paul calls us to be subject to the governing authorities, *whoever* they may be. That includes paying taxes you rightfully owe. When you make tax reduction a priority, you may be circumventing this command—whether you realize it or not.

Consider consulting a tax professional to make sure you are using every opportunity to save money. But don't expect miracles, and don't make tax reduction a top priority. That will only cause greater problems in the long run.

Action Item: Let's face it: Taxes, like death, are a fact of life. As long as you're meeting your Biblical responsibility to "render . . . to all their due," there's nothing wrong with making sure that you're paying no more taxes than is required. How confident are you that you're doing so? Perhaps you have a friend who's an accountant or tax preparer who could give you helpful advice for next year.

TODAY'S BOTTOM LINE
As Christians we are Biblically responsible to pay our fair share of taxes— no more and no less.

A Strategy That Works

Read
Proverbs 23:4-5

Session 4 has helped us get a handle on cutting our expenses (living, debt, and taxes) so that we can increase our cash flow. Now we must ask a key question: Why?

Why do we need more money? Perhaps that's a foolish question. But we need to answer it honestly.

As stewards we are responsible to manage prudently the resources God has given us. This involves investing.

What is an investment? *Something you put money into that is growing in value or has an economic return.* Therefore, a car is almost never an investment. Rarely does it grow in value or have an economic return. A home may fulfill that definition, but its primary purpose is not to make money but to provide shelter. Follow the Sequential Investment Strategy step by step (see page 73 in the *Workbook*) and you can grow prudently rather than jumping ahead into risky ventures you're not prepared to take.

Remember the parable of the talents (Matthew 25:14-30)? God obviously prizes diligence and ingenuity in investing His resources so that they expand and grow.

Even so, we need to step back and gain some perspective on investing. While God encourages us to be wise managers, He also wants us to maintain balance in pursuing our financial goals. So here's a timely reminder from His Word to meditate on: *Do not overwork to be rich; because of your own understanding, cease! Will you set your eyes on that which is not? For riches certainly make themselves wings; they fly away like an eagle toward heaven (Proverbs 23:4-5).*

And this: *A faithful man will abound with blessings, but he who hastens to be rich will not go unpunished (Proverbs 28:20).*

God's priorities are clear. There's no get-rich-quick scheme in the Bible you can follow. If you pursue money, it will only fly away from you faster. And lead you down paths that head toward destruction.

Instead, God calls for faithfulness. Is that *your* top priority?

Action Item: Look again at the Sequential Investment Strategy on page 73 in the *Workbook*. Evaluate any investments you have currently. Where do they fit in the steps? Have you taken any steps out of sequence? What actions will you take to get started properly with step one? Close your time with God by meditating on the verses above. Then ask Him to help you become even more faithful through the process of financial planning.

TODAY'S BOTTOM LINE

Investments of excess cash flow should be made with a sound strategy, pure motives, and diligent faithfulness.

A God of Order

DAY 1

SESSION 5

Read
1 Corinthians 14:40

Your parents or grandparents may have followed a time-honored means of money management you rarely see these days: A cookie jar.

Actually, the principles behind the cookie jar are sound:

First, with a cookie jar, *income is preallocated.* The money was used for specific purposes: life's necessities.

Second, *you're forced to stop spending money when the cookie jar is empty.*

Third, with a cookie jar *you always know where you are.* Just open the jar and count.

If you follow these three principles in a cash control system, you'll be well on your way to becoming an effective steward.

But let's step back a moment. Why is this financial orderliness so important?

Well, it's part of being a good steward—and we're taking Step 4 on the path to financial freedom: controlling and managing the cash flow you've been able to increase as a result of Step 3.

But there's a deeper, more significant reason. What is it?

God is a God of order. And He calls us to keep our lives in order, organized and efficient, so that we can truly fulfill our responsibility as stewards of His resources.

As the Apostle Paul put it, *Let all things be done decently and in order* (1 Corinthians 14:40).

When you care enough to do things in a thoughtful, orderly way, it indicates that what you are doing is important to you. It matters. If it didn't, you wouldn't think twice about how you did it. And as a steward, your financial affairs are certainly an important part of your life, worthy of your careful and orderly attention.

The problem is, many people come to this point in the process and give up. It can be tough to change stubborn habits, to set up a brand new system of finances, and to keep it going smoothly.

And yet, with God's grace, you can do that. Once you get over the start-up hump, you'll find it's a pleasure to keep this well-oiled engine running well.

Action Item: Look up the word "order" in a Bible concordance. Trace the concept of setting things "in order" throughout the Scriptures. Pay special attention to the importance of orderliness in the rituals of Exodus and Leviticus (as in Exodus 39:37; 40:4; 40:23; Leviticus 1:7-8,12; 6:12). Orderliness clearly is part of the image of God that He wants us to live out. If it's an area you struggle with, make it a matter of prayer right now.

TODAY'S BOTTOM LINE

Good stewardship requires an effective cash control system reflecting the orderliness God values.

Reward of the Diligent

In order to put a cash control system in place, you must accomplish four steps. Let's think again through those crucial steps:

1. Establish a Plan. By now you've worked through the forms in your *Workbook* to get started on this.

2. As*sign Responsibility.* Each partner should have clearly delineated responsibilities. The wife may be responsible for food and clothing budgets, and the husband for home and automotive expenses.

3. Record What Actually Happens. Keep track to determine how closely your actual expenses are to your estimates. This process alone will help you control spending.

4. Evaluate and Revise as Needed. Make any changes necessary to keep your cash control system as close to reality as possible.

It's one thing to follow four steps. It's another thing to develop the two important ingredients necessary for success: *diligence* and *flexibility.*

You need *diligence* to take the steps required. Let's face it, this is work. However, once your budget is established, it shouldn't require more than 20 to 30 minutes over an entire week. And the benefits are more than worth the effort.

And you need *flexibility* to keep the budget from being carved in stone, thus causing endless frustra-

tion. A budget is never the law, but rather a guide.

Here's an encouraging verse from Proverbs to meditate on: *The soul of a sluggard desires, and has nothing; but the soul of the diligent shall be made rich (Proverbs 13:4).*

You see, a lazy, disorganized person will never achieve financial freedom, but will instead be strapped by a continual desire for more. A desire that will never be satisfied because of his inability to work efficiently enough to reach it.

On the other hand, *the diligent shall be made rich.* Right? Well, we may wish it said that. But the promise is much more significant than that: *The soul of the diligent shall be made rich.*

That is the Biblical definition of financial freedom—when your soul is freed to experience the joy of good stewardship, no matter what your income may be.

Action Item: Assuming you've established your budget, take time right now to prayerfully—yes, prayerfully—review it. Ask God for the diligence and flexibility you need to fulfill the process. Then copy Proverbs 13:4 on a 3x5 card and tape it where you can see it next time you work on your budget.

TODAY'S BOTTOM LINE

An effective cash control system requires diligence and flexibility, but the effort is worth it all.

Talk Isn't Cheap

DAY 3
SESSION
5

Read
1 Corinthians 1:10

One time a lady approached Ron Blue and said, "My husband and I read *Master Your Money*." Ron immediately felt a sense of elation. Here was a fan! Until the woman continued: "I just have to tell you that book has caused me a great deal of frustration!" Ouch!

As a child, she explained, her parents had always given her any money she needed, and never required her to be accountable for it. After she'd married, her husband did the same. In fact, she'd never even written an entry in her checkbook register—she just wrote checks! How did she know how much she had in her account? "Well, the bank tells me every month, so I don't need to keep track of my checks!"

Obviously, getting her on a cash control system would be a challenge. But a deeper need became even more evident as she shared her struggles with Ron: the need for husband/wife communication.

Throughout this series we've stressed the importance of making your finances a partnership project. Of sharing your goals and dreams, and formulating a plan to reach them together. Finances often become a wedge between partners, rather than a bond that provides an encouraging impetus into the future together.

Perhaps now is the time for you to review what the Bible says about husbands and wives. Start with Ephesians 5:22-33, summarized in this verse: *Nevertheless let each one of you in particular so love his own wife as himself, and let the wife see that she respects her husband (Ephesians 5:33).*

And here's another verse you can apply to your marriage: *Now I plead with you, brethren, by the name of our Lord Jesus Christ, that you all speak the same thing, and that there be no divisions among you, but that you be perfectly joined together in the same mind and in the same judgment (1 Corinthians 1:10).*

If that verse is to be true anywhere, it should be true in Christian marriage.

Action Item: Russ Crosson, a colleague of Ron's, has written a helpful book: *Money and Your Marriage*. Russ includes a list of verses on communication. Take time to read and study these passages with your spouse: Genesis 2:18,21-24; Psalm 34:3; 128:1-4; Proverbs 5:18; 17:1; 17:14; Ecclesiastes 9:9; Malachi 2:16; Matthew 19:3-8; 1 Corinthians 1:10; 13:4-7; Ephesians 4:29; Philippians 2:2; Colossians 3:8-9; 4:6; 1 Timothy 3:4-5; Titus 1:6; 1 Peter 3:8-9; and James 1:19-20.

TODAY'S BOTTOM LINE

Marital communication that is open, honest, and harmonious is crucial to successful stewardship.

Stepping Ahead

DAY 4
SESSION 5

Read
Corinthians 9:24-27

Perhaps when you first saw the Financial Planning Flow Chart (see the back flap of the *Course Workbook*), it was a bit overwhelming. Hopefully that's not the case now!

That chart summarizes what we've been trying to learn through the "Master Your Money" series. It shows the various uses of income and the four steps to financial freedom as they relate to those uses.

Let's review the four steps you've taken through this series.

First, *you summarized your present situation.* You completed a Personal Balance Sheet after listing your assets and liabilities.

Second, *you established financial goals.* Together (if you're married) you set your long-range objectives and determined where you wanted to go financially.

Third, *you increased your cash flow margin.* You carefully reviewed your spending for living expenses, debt, and taxes to find areas you could cut back to increase your cash flow. That will fund long-range goals.

Fourth, *you began to control your cash flow.* By using a budget, you'll maintain control over your short-range spending in order to keep funding your margin and ultimately your long-range goals.

Now the goal is set before you; the finish line brings financial freedom. Paul challenges us: *Do you not know that those who run in a race all run, but one receives the prize? Run in such a way that you may obtain it. And everyone who competes for the prize is temperate in all things. Now they do it to obtain a perishable crown, but we for an imperishable crown. Therefore I run thus: not with uncertainty. Thus I fight: not as one who beats the air. But I discipline my body and bring it into subjection, lest, when I have preached to others, I myself should become disqualified (1 Corinthians 9:24-27).*

Let those words of exhortation be a guide for you, not just in your financial affairs, but in every aspect of your life as a steward of all of God's resources.

Run with certainty. Fight with purpose. And receive the imperishable crown God promises. The finish line is just ahead. Go for it!

Action Item: As you review the four steps we've taken, ask yourself which was the easiest one to take, and which was the hardest. Over time, you'll find the specific methods and systems that work best with you. As long as they follow the underlying principles, that's fine. These truths are meant to set you free, not restrict you. Close your time by praying for God's continuing guidance through the process.

TODAY'S BOTTOM LINE

A cash flow management system is the final step on the path to financial freedom for God's stewards

A Big Difference

DAY 5

SESSION

5

Read
Luke 12:15

You've learned a lot of helpful information. Now, what will you do with it? What is your overarching purpose for getting your finances in order?

Is it to achieve *financial success* or *financial freedom?*

There's a big difference. Some people manage their resources admirably, set aside plenty for long-range goals, and look forward to a comfortable retirement. They are financially successful. But unless they have the proper perspective, there's an emptiness, a futility, that pervades their lives, no matter how huge their balance sheet is.

But many others are experiencing true financial freedom. Their income may be much less in comparison; they may not have the trappings of success. But their priorities are set Biblically.

What's the difference? It all boils down to *motive.*

If you approach these principles solely with the motive of becoming wealthy, you will never experience contentment. But if you seek to serve God wholeheartedly through every resource He has entrusted to you, then you are on the pathway to financial freedom.

That doesn't mean we're "free" to buy or do anything we wish. Financial freedom is much richer than that; it's obeying God's will and experiencing His provision.

Remember that verse from Luke's gospel? *And [Jesus] said to them, "Take heed and beware of covetousness, for one's life does not consist in the abundance of the things he possesses" (Luke 12:15).*

That's a reminder to all of us who live in a world careening out of control in pursuit of pleasure, happiness, and fulfillment. The very attitude the world shuns—a humble acknowledgment of God's ownership of everything—is the only avenue to true contentment.

In our last session we'll focus on the privilege God gives His children to become involved financially in the work of His Kingdom. That's the priority that puts our lives as stewards into perspective.

Action Item: Fold a sheet of paper in half. On the left half, list your tangible possessions: house, cars, furniture. On the right, jot down some of the intangible aspects of life you enjoy: spouse, family, fellowship, relationship with God. Spend at least 10 minutes compiling your lists. Then open up your paper and compare the length of your two lists. In light of Luke 12:15, which list is more important to you? Which list would you like to see grow in the days ahead?

TODAY'S BOTTOM LINE

Financial freedom is reached only when our purpose is to serve God wholeheartedly utilizing all our resources.

The Neglected Priority

Here are some statistics to think about:
- More money is spent on chewing gum or dog food in the United States than is given to foreign missions.
- Americans on average give less than 1.7% of their adjusted gross income as charitable contributions.

Of course, giving by Christians would be much higher than that, right? Wrong:
- The average Christian gives approximately 2%!

Clearly, something is amiss here.

Without doubt, a major reason for the weakness of the church in the world today is that her members are not as involved as they should be in financially supporting the Lord's work.

Giving is the neglected priority.

Two misconceptions about giving cause even more confusion.

First, giving is not a *return* to God of His portion; rather it's a *recognition* of His ownership of all. As God told Job, "*Who has preceded Me, that I should pay him? Everything under heaven is Mine*" (*Job 41:11*).

If you think God will repay you just because you gave to His work, think again; He already owns everything!

You see, we give not because He needs the money, but because we recognize our responsibility to honor and obey Him.

Second, giving isn't a *cause* of spiritual growth, it's a *consequence* of spiritual growth.

Giving breaks money's power over people, because when you give you voluntarily lose control of it. If you cannot give it up, then you don't own it, it owns you.

As you read these devotions this week, keep in mind the challenge of Session 6: Make giving a priority in your life, the ultimate purpose for your financial planning.

What could God do with a church of obedient stewards who give generously of His resources to the work of His Kingdom? The answer to that question would boggle the mind. And shake the world.

Action Item: Find last year's tax return or do some digging through your receipts and check stubs to determine just how much you gave to the Lord's work in the past year. What percentage of your gross income does that represent? In light of what we're learning, where is giving on your list of priorities? Close your time today by praying that God would soften your heart toward Him, so that you will be fully open to His will regarding the priority of giving.

TODAY'S BOTTOM LINE

Giving is a top priority for Christians because it recognizes God's ownership of all things.

Excuses, Excuses

DAY 2

SESSION

6

Read
Proverbs 3:9

Honor the Lord with your possessions, and with the first-fruits of all your increase (Proverbs 3:9).

The Old Testament saint took that command literally. In fact, the Scriptures instructed him to make specific offerings and gifts to the Lord, starting with the tithe—10% of all he owned. But that's not where it ended. If you add up all the offerings the Old Testament saint was instructed to give to God's work, it was nearly 30% of his income!

So why do Christians today get stuck around 2%? Our priorities have certainly shifted!

There are some common reasons we don't give as we should.

First, *we don't know we can give* and still meet all our other goals and obligations. In other words, we've never analyzed all our financial resources to discover the full story of our obligations and opportunities. It's difficult to be a good steward if you don't know what you have. So, to be safe, we avoid giving.

Second, *we don't know how to give.* We're not aware of all the various ways to give, such as giving appreciated property, certain tangible assets, corporate stocks, trusts or charitable foundations. Most people need some guidance in these areas, but they can maximize

your giving if used properly.

Third, *we don't plan to give.* We live as responders rather than planners. With planning, the average person's giving increases about fourfold.

A well-known entrepreneur once said, "Anyone, especially a businessman, has more uses for money than the money available. Therefore, unless he *plans* to give, he never will give." If your lifestyle is consumptive, you can never accumulate enough to give substantially toward the cause of Christ.

Those are common reasons for not giving. But that doesn't mean they're acceptable! May God help you push aside all the obstacles to giving that have hindered you up until now.

Action Item: Select the primary reason you don't give as much as you'd like: either you don't know you can give, you don't know how to give, or you don't plan to give. What specific steps have you taken through this series to settle that issue? What further steps will you take to turn all those negative excuses into positive examples? If you're married, take some time this evening to talk about these questions with your spouse.

TODAY'S BOTTOM LINE

Despite the excuses we may make, God still calls His children to honor Him with their gifts.

3 Levels of Giving

DAY 3

SESSION

6

Read
1 Corinthians 16:2

A farmer promised to give the Lord one of the twin calves his cow delivered. His wife asked him, "Which calf is the Lord's?" He answered, "It really doesn't make any difference whose calf is whose. I'll give God one of them when they're grown."

A few weeks later he came into the farmhouse, sadness hanging on his face. His wife asked, "What's wrong?" He replied, "Well, the Lord's calf died this morning."

We may smile at that, but it's a typical attitude among Christians. Rather than grasping the concept that God owns it all, we tend to think it's all ours, and we'll give the Lord whatever we have left over . Which all too often isn't much.

In light of that, consider again the three levels of giving.

First is the *Should Give* level. This is proportionate giving: each Christian giving according to what he or she has received. *On the first day of the week let each one of you lay something aside, storing up as he may prosper, that there be no collections when I come (1 Corinthians 16:2).* Based on the Old Testament principle, the beginning point here should be a tithe—literally 10%.

Second is the *Could Give* level. This is planned giving: the amount we could give if we gave up something else. Perhaps if we pass up a vacation, a special savings account,

or a lifestyle desire, we can help accomplish something significant for the Lord. This brings to mind the widow's sacrificial gift: *"For all these out of their abundance have put in offerings for God, but she out of her poverty has put in all the livelihood that she had" (Luke 21:4).* Barnabas provides another example in Acts 4:36-37.

Third is the *Would Give* level. This is precommitted giving: we commit ourselves to giving if God provides a certain amount above and beyond what we could ever hope to give ourselves (see 2 Corinthians 9:6-15). Unless we are precommitted to give the surplus, we will spend it on something else.

Should give, could give, would give. Three levels of giving that will change your life.

Action Item: Evaluate each level of giving personally. First, where are you in the *Should Give* level? You determined that yesterday. Second, have you ever given in the *Could Give* level? What specific action could you take to do so? And third, have you prayed about what you *Would Give* by faith in God's provision? Record your answers on the Faith Giving Pledge (page 103 in the *Course Workbook*).

TODAY'S BOTTOM LINE

Giving has levels: what you should give by tithing, could give by sacrificing, and would give by God's provision.

Don't Miss It

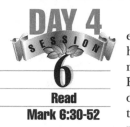

DAY 4

SESSION 6

Read
Mark 6:30-52

Jesus has entered into the height of His brief ministry on earth. His 12 followers are dispatched two-by-two to serve. And now, their assignment complete, they return to report to their Master.

And He said to them, "Come aside by yourselves to a deserted place and rest a while" (Mark 6:31). Why not "come aside" and read Mark 6:30-52. There are several key principles at work in this dramatic passage.

1. Spend time alone with God (6:31). The first step to financial freedom is to seek God's will through Bible reading and prayer.

2. Your commitment is to God, not your financial plans (6:34). Jesus planned to go with His disciples to a quiet place. But, confronted by the people's needs, He responded to God's direction. Let God be free to break into your plans.

3. Practical advice may not be the right advice (6:35-36). The disciples came to Jesus with a smart idea, but not the right idea. Be discerning in regard to the world's advice.

4. Giving will never make economic sense (6:37). Jesus told the disciples to feed the multitudes. That made no sense to them. In the same way, giving never makes financial sense. At least to the world.

5. God uses what you have, not what you don't have (6:38). They started with five loaves and two fish.

They didn't go beyond what they had—that was their starting point.

6. God's ways are not our ways (6:39-44). They had 12 baskets full of leftovers! That's God's compounding. It's incomprehensible. But He's an incomparable God.

7. God will never leave you nor forsake you (6:45-50). In the disciples' time of need, Jesus was there. Miraculously.

8. Don't miss the miracle God has for you (6:51-52). The disciples' hearts were hardened to God working miraculously in their lives.

Don't let that happen to you. Whatever God is telling you to do—get out of debt, increase your giving sacrificially, improve your communication with your spouse—do it, by faith. Take the step. Don't miss the miracle God has for you.

Action Item: Maybe God is impressing on you that you have not been as good a steward of His resources as you could be. If so, ask Him for forgiveness right now. Purpose in your heart to begin today the process of becoming a faithful steward. If you're married, discuss this commitment with your spouse. Ask your pastor or a trusted friend to hold you accountable for the steps you need to take.

TODAY'S BOTTOM LINE

God is ready to work miracles through the life of an obedient, willing steward who walks with Him daily.

Judgment Day

Read
2 Corinthians 5:10

For we must all appear before the judgment seat of Christ, that each one may receive the things done in the body, according to what he has done, whether good or bad (2 Corinthians 5:10).

Ever wondered what it will be like to stand before the Lord Jesus Christ and have Him evaluate your works? To hear His commendation . . . or to watch as most of the works you have performed are consumed by fire (see 1 Corinthians 3:11-15)?

The reason we've produced the "Master Your Money" Video Series is to give you the guidance you need from God's Word to understand His will for you as a faithful steward of His resources.

We've learned many principles and practices to help you experience financial freedom, God's way. We've filled out plenty of worksheets to help you get a handle on where you are, where you're going, and how to manage your resources profitably. And we've challenged you to reassess your giving to the Lord's work—the most important use of your money.

Yet it all falls apart if these principles and practices are not built on a solid relationship with the Lord. You cannot be a responsible steward if you do not know the Master personally, continually building your relationship with Him.

That takes spending time every day with Him, reading His Word and praying. If you've been using this devotional guide regularly, you've already spent 30 days developing the habit. Now, keep going. Walk Thru the Bible offers several exciting and practical devotional guides (see the inside back cover for information). Consider using one of them in your daily journey with the Lord.

Fellow steward, continue to follow faithfully His will for you. Dedicate yourself to be a wise steward of all God's resources, in every area of life. Then, when you stand before your gracious, loving Lord at the judgment seat, you can hear Him say to you, *"Well done, good and faithful servant; you were faithful over a few things, I will make you ruler over many things. Enter into the joy of your lord"* (Matthew 25:21).

Action Item: On a sheet of paper with two columns, write in the left column the three most important insights you've learned from participating in this series. Then in the right column, jot down how each insight will change the way you live. In prayer, commit yourself to God to do the best you can to fulfill His calling on you as His "good and faithful" steward.

TODAY'S BOTTOM LINE

The godly steward will experience financial freedom on earth and earn the Lord's commendation in heaven.

WALK THRU THE BIBLE MINISTRIES

From their international headquarters in Atlanta, Georgia, the multifaceted ministries of Walk Thru the Bible reach around the world, helping Christians build their lives on the firm foundation of God's Word.

Since 1976 WTB has grown to encompass these major ministries:

■ *Walk Thru the Old and New Testament/400 Silent Years Seminars.* Developed by Dr. Bruce Wilkinson, these life-changing seminars help participants gain the big picture of God's Word through ingenious memorization techniques. This practical overview enables Christians to understand the chronology, geography, characters, and themes of the Bible so they feel more "at home" in the Word than ever before. As a result, attendees become excited about and committed to reading God's Word. More than 1,000 WTB seminars are taught each year by nearly 200 instructors in more than two dozen countries worldwide.

■ *Devotional Publications.* WTB's nationally renowned devotional guides are practical, contemporary tools designed to help believers gain strength by reading God's Word daily. As a result, their lives are anchored to the rock of truth, and God's relevant message goes with them throughout their day. Today, over half a million copies of WTB devotional guides are published every month.

■ *Video Ministry.* WTB offers several extensive courses featuring outstanding communicators on video, including series on marriage, leadership, and finances.

■ *Applied Principles of Learning.* This outstanding video/live teaching curriculum offers unique training for Christian communicators of all kinds, helping them improve their skills so they can teach Biblical truth for lifechange. The APL Curriculum includes two separate courses: "The 7 Laws of the Learner" by Dr. Bruce Wilkinson, and "The 7 Laws of the Teacher" by Dr. Howard G. Hendricks, Christian educator, author, and communicator.

■ *Other Ministries. Atlanta Area Ministries* offers Bible studies throughout the Metro area. *The Study Tours Ministry* leads pilgrims on sojourns annually to the Holy Land. *The International Ministry* sends Walk Thru the Bible into two dozen countries around the world.

Walk Thru the Bible is ministering for lifechange in creative, Biblical ways. Feel free to contact us for more information on any of our ministries.

Walk Thru the Bible Ministries®
61 Perimeter Park N.E.
P.O. Box 80587
Atlanta, Georgia 30366
Telephone 800-554-9300
(In Georgia: 404-458-9300)

Walk Thru the Bible Ministries is a member of the Evangelical Council for Financial Accountability.